HONEY

Sascha Wassermann-Kremen

Presentation by *BookLeaf Publishing*

Web: www.bookleafpub.com

E-mail: info@bookleafpub.com

ISBN: 9789357614597

First edition 2022

To all the lonely souls looking for some company.

ACKNOWLEDGEMENT

Thank you to my parents for constantly pushing me to explore my creativity and standing by me no matter what. Thank you to all of the teachers who saw something in me, even a glimmer of hope that was worth pursuing. Thank you to my fantastic partner Lena for loving me when I truly needed it most and never failing to push me when I would have given up. None of this would have been possible without all of you and I'm forever grateful.

ONE

She was draped in sadness, protected from the unknown that awaited her pin pricked pupils.

There goes that itch again, the one you can never scratch, there's that gaping hole that you've always had and will forever continue to fill.

She lets it soak into every crevice of her damaged, lilac body like that dirty old sponge crawling with deceit that's stuck to the bottom of the sink.

If you've never walked down the forbidden road, the dark and dingy escape from reality you wouldn't know pure bliss and total fucking ecstasy if it smacked you in the face.

I watched the trains charge off into the skyline to never be seen again, the layers of rust and patches of oil disguising each carriage as the clouds came apart.

Who doesn't love watching the dark thick sea engulf the sun just so it can spit it back out again hours later, the colours changing as she wets her brush and splattered the sunrise across the sky.

TWO

A hundred thousand sunsets ago the air smelt
different, it felt like a cigarette being lit by a
match- burning the tip until that first breath of
smoke charred your throat.

Her gaze was all consuming, when she pursed
her lips together it made my knees weak, she
was more beautiful than any collection of words
I'd ever hoped to write and that hint of
narcissism kept me on my toes as she spun webs
in the depths of my harrowing mind.

With every twist and turn spinning me into
oblivion, the building stretched taller and the
roads longer, with little to no purity left in my
brittle bones I made it my mission to perfume
myself with the scent of nicotine and rat poison.

THREE

The morning glare was blinding

The air was icy, cold killing

I collapsed into her warm embrace as the ocean
continued to kiss the shell covered shores

The days went past with out a single doubt

Numbing my mind was the only way through
the storm that was my life

You're nothing until the stars guide the moon to
safety

A sad glimpse of your past, the realisation so
paralysing you wish you didn't carry every
ounce of the worlds sorrow on your shoulders

Universes lacing the atmosphere that we're all
blind to, each and every thought became a word
coating our planet

FOUR

I think of her when the clouds pass by

The sky's a dream, a colour pallet of lust

She's too kind hearted for this unforgiving
world, her heart beat is the only drum I march to
and her eyes are a whole other dimension

I wont let her gaze into my soul, she's a marvel
and I cannot breathe when she looks at me

She stands tall like the trees hovering over the
dirt, like the sky scrapers closing in on the city

The absolute pleasure of watching her blossom
like a flower in the wind, there's nothing and no
one I'd rather feel the sky change with

FIVE

The wet grass on a cold morning, the cool sand touching your toes on a scorching afternoon, that slight breeze that lifts the dead leaves off the trees and everything in between.

Those memories are all we have when we centre ourselves inside our heads, the clocks keep ticking and the tides keep turning.

How many thoughts stream through the river of our minds as we anxiously await for all the individual worlds to implode?

No pattern or presence can put our anxieties at ease, we all crave objects and possessions for that simple dopamine hit and all anyone is left with are the creepy crawlies that linger at night and hide in the crevices no human wants to acknowledge.

SIX

There's a river of doubt flowing through each one of us, it drips out like an icicle slowly melting away from the suns beaming pulses of life.

We each lie in bed as the moon glistens on the oceans face, as all of our thoughts (from rational to chaotic) clump together and leave each and everyone of us breathless, some doze into a deep world we barely remember and others toss and turn as the horrific state of nostalgia seeps in.

The man who was in front of you that morning buying coffee blasted classical music to drown out the world and all its inhabitants, the woman you accidentally bumped into going into the bathroom was so deeply immersed in her phone that she pulsated as she moved like a glitching hologram about to crackle into nothing.

Our lives are constructed by our interactions with people, unnoticed and stored in the deep folds of our rotting brains, locking our abysmal selves in rooms surrounded by more rooms so we feel a sense of relief from the extreme energy surging around outside.

SEVEN

My desperate cries were to be heard by no one,
the endless echo of my aching heart was nothing
but a whimper in the worlds ears.

I splashed my reflection out of the crystal clear
puddle and tried to recall my face as it once was,
broken mirrors and umbrellas open inside are
how everyone must think of me.

The lightening cracked the sky open and it bled
onto the trees turning them a deep vermillion,
the thunder roared piercing every ear drum
across the tranquil planet, the rain poured harder
than a tropical storm and before I could take one
step the wind started to twirl me like a ballerina
in her final performance.

The rain of a thousand days is all I dream of,
drowning the city and consuming every last
brick and nail, Atlantis doesn't seem so mythical
after all.

EIGHT

The sun keeps chasing the moon around my life
like children having fun, a timelapse of all my
moments would be the easy way out.

I want to transform every second into an
exquisite jumble of words until my fingers
bleed, to help other lost souls travel to the places
of their dreams.

I grind my teeth constantly without really taking
any notice, hitting the keys on my keyboard like
I'm playing a symphony that resonates as pure
chaos.

NINE

A reflection of the stage above our sleepy minds
glistens and dances as we count down the
sunrise,

The town fades away like it never existed as we
stroll further into the fluorescent shimmer that
may engulf our decrepit legs,

The stench of rotting wood fused with a
thousand creeks swaying with the earths breath,

To capture the elusive sky that holds us all in
place will only ever be a sleeting thought.

TEN

I spy with my little eye, only through this
distorted lens of mine

Someone frozen in time, once again

Each drop noticed and needed

I captured the smell, the absolute essence of that
moment

I trapped it and tried to call it my own

Just so someone could rip it away from my
blood soaked eyes

ELEVEN

The furious snow casting its immensely
ungrateful shadow upon me

Sleek and slender buildings tower over my
shoulder like a predator about to pounce

Things are twisting around tomorrow's horizons,
choking them pale blue as if its a dreary Sunday
morning

The absolute agony gives me a rush, its pure
bliss and the complete heroin of it all is
priceless. Don't stop.

The overflow tank is blacked up with emotions
leaving nowhere for the river of glutinous tar
that surrounds my soul

The selfishness and savageness contained in our
atmosphere ices over me-
Purifying the temptress our world truly is.

Shes a stalker of sorts, watching and waiting for
those walls to start crumbling

It's almost like being admired in a twisted way
but I'd rather be totally isolated on a day like
today.

TWELVE

The coldness crept through the suns first glance
of the morning like the harrowing eyes of
someone peering over a cliffs edge

The ultimate gift of walking to snow falling
from a different worlds sky is galactic
-and when the smallest ray of sun hits even a
snow flake
It's blinding.

Nothing else mattered in those moments, the
concreteness gave me a pedestal to start my day
on

By the time a full colour pallet was visible in the
skyline
The consciousness surrounding me far and wide
was alive, breathing everything in.

THIRTEEN

Day after day we continue to rinse yesterday's
filth and regret off ourselves,
The hope that your own despicable flesh and
blood will be loved, adored and punished
glooms over each one of us

The cruelness and constant criticism always
manages to captivate my washed out brain, some
lucky piece of flesh will stumble across this
appalling excuse of a human being and while my
tears fall like the leaves of a hundred trees - all
my vices failed to fix me and you will too.

Your pretty little precious heart will break for
me when I'm as good as dead yet again, shoe
laces tying my life together like i never could
and all the miserable bodies roam this distraught
planet
- plagued by hatred and driven by greatness.

FOURTEEN

You're my absolute fascination and deliver every
sort of sensation,
You demand attention like the brightest stars in
the sky seek validation,
The clouds pass by in all shapes and sizes which
create new dreams that come only draped in
silence,
So deep in your shadow I can never see myself
and now all of sudden the universe cares about
your mental health?
Double rainbows, fairy floss fun but what about
who you'll become?
Losing sleep caught in this twilight of bliss will
always keep the pain away but the final
goodnight kiss isn't ever too far away.

FIFTEEN

This is just to say

My mind
flickers like a
camera capturing
all the rain
drops that
will never reach
the ground.

With my back
to the
thumping speaker, I
feel my
corroding heart beat
slowly sync
with the atmosphere
-The energy,
the pulsing energy
corses through
the veins of
the entire
club. We
are one just
for tonight

SIXTEEN

I'll chase you like the comets in the deepest areas
of space chase the sun,

You are my glass half empty that slowly soaks
every ocean dry,

Conquered cities eventually divide just like my
heart does,

The complete and utter vastness of the skies
impels me to exist as I am and no longer try to
change,

Your eyes are my salvation when a sea of
troubles consumes me, drowns me and infinitely
over powers me,

The clouds squeeze me dry of all possible
emotions while the skeletal carcasses of the
damned follow my every move,

Flashing lights on a busy city night surround the
cynical trees blowing in the late night wind and
like pictures speaking to me on a personal level,
every ounce of love and hate end up on the same
line.

SEVENTEEN

Why care for devotion when my heart can be
mended with any substance I soak my body in?

We continuously stretch each bit of horror out
like a rubber band and will it not to snap back in
our distorted faces

Clearer skies and broader perceptions are a
fantasy I do not have time for, even though we
all live by them

You are meant to caress me with good intentions
and yet you choke me carelessly. You reel me in
like a gigantic prized fish to only skin me alive
and pull my innards out for your grotesque
pleasure.

-Why thank you, here's your receipt!

EIGHTEEN

Pain always has its way of catching up with me,
when I look into his dull unaware eyes, that look
brings me to pieces and as hard as I try to sticky
tape it together
-my heart breaks for him.
He's left our realm for now and usually he
returns, but what if he smiles at me for the last
time?
I can't bare to see you kill yourself slowly,
you've slithered away from my safe embrace to
the only place I'm not allowed to enter.

Dazed and confused you tell me you love me,
that you're fine but he's got his claws in you and
they're in so deep that you're hanging your pure
beating heart from the heavens.

- Leaving it to shrivel and dry out (just like he's
always wanted)

www.ingramcontent.com/pod-product-compliance
Lightning Source LLC
Chambersburg PA
CBHW070736160726
48003CB00006BA/2537